THE YUKON POEMS
of
Robert W. Service

THE YUKON POEMS
of
Robert W. Service

ISBN: 1-57833-089-0
Drawings: Lisa Forbush
Typeface: Times
Book layout & design: Tina Wallace

Copyright 1999 Todd Communications

Published by Todd Communications
Anchorage, Juneau & Fairbanks, Alaska

To order additional copies of this book, please send
$4.95 (includes $1 postage and handling) to:

Todd Communications
203 W. 15th Ave. Suite 102
Anchorage, AK 99501
(907) 274- TODD (8633)
Fax (907) 276-6858
e-mail: sales@toddcom.com

Robert W. Service
1874 - 1958

Robert W. Service didn't arrive in Canada's Yukon until 1904 when the Rush of '98 had largely played out and most of the miners had frozen, starved or left the territory. But by seeing what remained and talking to those who stayed from his vantage point as a teller for what is now the Canadian Imperial Bank of Commerce, he was able to bring to life the trials and tribulations of thousands who sought gold in North America's greatest gold rush.

A native of Lancashire County, Service was born in Preston, England January 14, 1874 on the banks of the River Ribble about 25 miles north of Liverpool. He grew up in Glasgow, Scotland and upon graduation from school became apprenticed as a bank clerk. Like thousands of Scots before and after him, he became restless and headed for the beckoning shores of North America and ended up in Canada. By 1903 he had arrived on the west coast of the country in British Columbia and by the following year he had migrated farther north to work as a bank clerk in Whitehorse, the Yukon.

A short time later the bank transferred him to the larger community of Dawson City at the confluence of the Klondike and Yukon Rivers and the heart of the gold rush. He occupied a small cabin on a hill just outside of the heart of the city where he could see the meandering Yukon beyond the city streets. It is well preserved to this day and serves as a memorial to the poet of the north with daily recitations of his work by a skilled raconteur named Tom Byrne. This is an experience worth taking in if you ever make it to the former capital of the Yukon.

In addition to his duties at the bank, the clerk assiduously wrote verse so that by 1907 he had accumulated enough to have his poetry published in London under the name *Songs of a Sourdough.* That same year a Philadelphia, Pennsylvania publisher, Edward Stern and Company, also published the book, but under a different name: *The Spell of the Yukon and Other Verses.* The tome included such classics as "The Shooting of Dan McGrew" and "The Cremation of Sam McGee." All three of these favorites are contained in this brief booklet. Service's first published work was a rip roaring success in several editions and earned the earnest clerk enough in royalties to allow him to leave the bank in 1909. The same year Stern and Company published *"Ballads of a Cheechako*"* a lengthier collection of prose about charlatans, miners and ladies of the gold rush era.

At that time the Balkans were a trouble spot in Europe, much as they are today. Service took advantage of his publishing gains that far exceeded anything most of the miners made and in 1912 headed for that trouble spot as a war correspondent for the *Toronto Star* newspaper. After reporting on the Balkan War, he continued to travel extensively from the South Seas to France where he eventually settled down and married a French woman. From 1913 until his death in 1958 he spent most of his time in the balmy south of France, continuing to write poetry, five novels and a two-volume autobiography. During World War I in Europe he served with an American ambulance group and wrote *The Rhymes of a Red Cross Man*, which was a very popular expression of patriotism casting glory on the common foot soldier.

His novels include *The Trail of Ninety-Eight*; *A Northland Romance* in 1910; *The Poisoned Paradise* in 1922; *The Roughneck* in 1923; *The Master of the Microbe* in 1926 and *The House of Fear* in 1927. Volume I of his autobiography was published in 1945 and a second volume was published in 1948.

But by far his best known work was the recounting of the experiences of the gold rush of 1898 and the royalties from those poems helped sustain him for a lifetime. His style was much like that of Coleridge in "The Rime of the Ancient Mariner," favoring internal rhymes in prolonged verse. Service, an Englishman raised in Scotland, who made his fame and fortune in Canada during a gold rush manned largely by U.S. citizens, died in Lacieux, France September 11, 1958.

This brief tome contains five of the bard's most memorable and well known tales which generations of school children have read, memorized and passed down to the next generation.

*Cheechako is a northern term for a tenderfoot or newcomer to the north.

Contents

The Shooting of Dan McGrew

A bunch of the boys were whooping it up in the
      Malamute saloon;
The kid that handles the music-box was hitting a
      jag-time tune;
Back of the bar, in a solo game, sat Dangerous Dan
      McGrew,
And watching his luck was his light-o'-love, the
      lady that's known as Lou.

When out of the night, which was fifty-below, and
      into the din and the glare,
There stumbled a miner fresh from the creeks, dog-
      dirty, and loaded for bear.
He looked like a man with a foot in the grave and
      scarcely the strength of a louse.
Yet he tilted a poke of dust on the bar, and he called
      for drinks for the house.

There was none could place the stranger's face,
      though we searched ourselves for a clue;
But we drank to his health, and the last to drink was
      Dangerous Dan McGrew.

There's men that somehow just grip your eyes, and
      hold them hard like a spell;
And such was he, and he looked to me like a man
      who had lived in hell;
With a face most hair, and the dreary stare of a dog
      whose day is done,
As he watered the green stuff in his glass, and the
      drops fell one by one.
Then I got to figgering who he was, and wondering
      what he'd do,
And I turned my head — and there watching him
      was the lady that's known as Lou.
His eyes went rubbering around the room, and he
      seemed in a kind of daze,
Till at last that old piano fell in the way of his
      wandering gaze.

The rag-time kid was having a drink; there was no
      one else on the stool,
So the stranger stumbles across the room, and flops
      down there like a fool.
In a buckskin shirt that was glazed with dirt he sat,
      and I saw him sway;
Then he clutched the keys with his talon hands —
      my God! but that man could play.

Were you ever out in the Great Alone, when the
      moon was awful clear,
And the icy mountains hemmed you in with a
      silence you most could *hear*;
With only the howl of a timber wolf, and you
      camped there in the cold,
A half-dead thing in a stark, dead world, clean mad
      for the muck called gold;
While high overhead, green, yellow and red, the
      North Lights swept in bars? —
Then you've a haunch what the music meant . . .
      hunger and night and the stars.

And hunger not of the belly kind, that's banished
      with bacon and beans,
But with the gnawing hunger of lonely men for a
      home and all that it means;
For a fireside far from the cares that are, four walls
      and a roof above;
But oh! so cramful of cosy joy, and crowned with a
      woman's love —
A woman dearer than all the world, and true as
      Heaven is true —
(God! how ghastly she looks through her rouge, —
      the lady that's known as Lou.)

Then on a sudden the music changed, so soft that
      you scarce could hear;
But you felt that your life had been looted clean of
      all that it once held dear;
That someone had stolen the women you loved; that
      her love was a devil's lie;

That your guts were gone, and the best for you was
        to crawl away and die.
'Twas the crowning cry of a heart's despair, and it
        thrilled you through and through —
"I guess I'll make it a spread misere*," said
        Dangerous Dan McGrew.

The music almost died away . . . then it burst like a
        pent-up flood;
And it seemed to say, "Repay, repay," and my eyes
        were blind with blood.
The thought came back of an ancient wrong, and it
        stung like a frozen lash,
And the lust awoke to kill, to kill . . . then the music
        stopped with a crash,
And the stranger turned, and his eyes they burned in
        a most peculiar way;
In a buckskin shirt that was glazed with dirt he sat,
        and I saw him sway;
Then his lips went in a kind of grin, and he spoke,
        and his voice was calm,
And "Boys," says he, "you don't know me, and
        none of you care a damn;
But I want to state, and my words are straight, and
        I'll bet my poke they're true,
That one of you is a hound of hell . . . and that one
        is Dan McGrew."

Then I ducked my head, and the lights went out, and
        two guns blazed in the dark,

*spread misere - gold rush card game in which the player
shows cards face up and is trying to lose every trick.

And a woman screamed, and the lights went up, and
two men lay stiff and stark.
Pitched on his head, and pumped full of lead, was
Dangerous Dan McGrew,
While the man from the creeks lay clutched to the
breast of a lady that's known as Lou.

These are the simple facts of the case, and I guess I
ought to know.
They say that the stranger was crazed with "hooch"
and I'm not denying it's so.
I'm not so wise as the lawyer guys, but strictly
between us two —
The woman that kissed him and — pinched his
pole — was the lady that's know as Lou.

The Law of the Yukon

This is the law of the Yukon, and ever she makes it
      plain;
"Send not your foolish and feeble; send me your
      strong and your sane —
Strong for the red courage of battle; sane, for I harry
      them sore;
Send me men girt for the combat, men who are grit
      to the core;
Swift as the panther in triumph, fierce as the bear in
      defeat,
Sired of a bulldog parent, steeled in the furnace
      heat.
Send me the best of your breeding, lend me your
      chosen ones;
Them will I take to my bosom, them will I call my
      sons;
Them will I gild with my treasure, them will I glut
      with my meat;

But the others — the misfits, the failures — I trample
      under my feet.
Dissolute, damned and despairful, crippled and
      palsied and slain,
Ye would send me the spawn of your gutters — Go!
      take back your spawn again.

"Wild and wide are my borders, stern as death is my
      sway;
From my ruthless throne I have ruled alone for a
      million years and a day;
Hugging my mighty treasure, waiting for man
      to come,
Till he swept like a turbid torrent, and after him
      swept — the scum.
The pallid pimp of the dead-line, the enervate
      of the pen.
One by one I weeded them out, for all that I sought
      was — Men.
One by one I dismayed them, frightening them sore
      with my glooms;
One by one I betrayed them unto my manifold dooms.

Drowned them like rats in my rivers, starved them like
      curs on my plains,
Rotted the flesh that was left them, poisoned the blood
      in their veins;
Burst with my winter upon them, searing forever
      their sight,
Lashed them with fungus-white faces, whimpering
      wild in the night;

Staggering blind through the storm-whirl, stumbling
        mad through the snow,
Frozen stiff in the ice-pack, brittle and bent like a bow;
Featureless, formless, forsaken, scented by wolves in
        their flight,
Left for the wind to make music through ribs that are
        glittering white;
Gnawing the black crust of failure, searching the
        pit of dispair,
Crooking the toe in the trigger, trying to patter a
        prayer;
Going outside with an escort, raving with lips all
        afoam,
Writing a cheque for a million, driveling feebly of
        home;
Lost like a louse in the burning . . . or else in the
        tented town
Seeking a drunkard's solace, sinking and sinking
        down;
Steeped in the slime at the bottom, dead to a decent
        world,

Lost 'mid the human flotsam, far on the frontier
    hurled;
In the camp at the bend of the river, with its dozen
    saloons aglare,
Its gambling dens ariot, its gramophones all ablare;
Crimped with the crimes of a city, sin-ridden and
    bridled with lies,
In the hush of my mountained vastness, in the flush
    of my midnight skies.
Plaque-spots, yet tools of my purpose, so natheless* I
    suffer them thrive,
Crushing my Weak in their clutches, that only my
    Strong may survive.

"But the others, the men of my mettle, the men who
    would 'stablish my fame
Unto its ultimate issue, winning me honor,
    not shame;
Searching my uttermost valleys, fighting each step as
    they go,
Shooting the wrath of my rapids, scaling my ramparts
    of snow;
Ripping the guts of my mountains, looting the beds
    of my creeks,
Them will I take to my bosom, and speak as a
    mother speaks.

I am the land that listens, I am the land that broods;
Steeped in eternal beauty, crystalline waters and
    woods.

*never the less

Long have I waited lonely, shunned as a thing
      accurst,
Monstrous, moody, pathetic, the last of the lands
      and the first;
Visioning camp-fires at twilight, sad with a longing
      forlorn,
Feeling my womb o'er-pregnant with the seed of
      cities unborn.
Wild and wide are my borders, stern as death is my
      sway,

And I wait for the men who will win me — and I will
      not be won in a day;
And I will not be won by weaklings, subtle, suave
      and mild,
But by men with hearts of vikings, and the
      simple faith of a child;
Desperate, strong and resistless, unthrottled by fear
      or defeat,
Them, will I gild with my treasure, them will I glut
      with my meat.

"Lofty I stand from each sister land, patient and
      wearily wise,
With the weight of a world of sadness in my quiet,
      passionless eyes;
Dreaming alone of a people, dreaming alone
      of a day,
When men shall not rape my riches, and curse me
      and go away;

Making a bawd of my bounty, fouling the hand that
gave —
Till I rise in my wrath and I sweep on their path and
I stamp them into a grave.
Dreaming of men who will bless me, of women
esteeming me good,

Of children born in my borders of radiant
motherhood,
Of cities leaping to stature, of fame like a flag
unfurled,
As I pour the tide of my riches in the eager lap of
the world."

The is the Law of the Yukon, that only the Strong
shall thrive;
That surely the Weak shall perish, and only the Fit
survive.
Dissolute, damned and despairful, crippled and
palsied and slain,
This is the Will of the Yukon, — Lo, how she makes
it plain!

The Cremation of Sam McGee

There are strange things done in the midnight sun
by the men who moil for gold;
The Arctic trails have their secret tales
That would make your blood run cold;
The Northern Lights have seen queer sights,
But the queerest they ever did see
Was that night on the marge of Lake Lebarge
I cremated Sam McGee.

Now Sam McGee was from Tennessee, where the
  cotton blooms and blows.
Why he left his home in the South to roam 'round
  the Pole, God only knows.

He was always cold, but the land of gold seemed
        to hold him like a spell;
Though he'd often say in his homely way that
        "he'd sooner live in hell."

On a Christmas Day we were mushing our way over
        the Dawson trail.
Talk of your cold! through the parka's fold it
        stabbed like a driven nail.
If our eyes we'd close, then the lashes froze till
        sometimes we couldn't see;
It wasn't much fun, but the only one to whimper
        was Sam McGee.

And that very night, as we lay packed tight in our
        robes beneath the snow,
And the dogs were fed, and the stars o'erhead were
        dancing heel and toe,
He turned to me, and "Cap," says he, "I'll cash in
        this trip, I guess;
And if I do, I'm asking that you won't refuse my
        last request."

Well, he seemed so low that I couldn't say no; then
        he says with a sort of moan:
"It's the cursed cold, and it's got right hold till I'm
        chilled clean through to the bone.

Yet 'tain't being dead — it's my awful dread of the
        icy grave that pains;
So I want you to swear that, foul or fair, you'll
        cremate my last remains."

A pal's last need is a thing to heed, so I swore I
        would not fail;
And we started on at the streak of dawn; but God!
        he looked ghastly pale.
He crouched on the sleigh, and he raved all day of
        his home in Tennessee;
And before nightfall a corpse was all that was left of
        Sam McGee.

There wasn't a breath in that land of death, and I
        hurried, horror-driven,
With a corpse half hid that I couldn't get rid,
        because of a promise given;
It was lashed to the sleigh, and it seemed to say:
        "You may tax your brawn and brains,
But you promised true, and it's up to you to cremate
        those last remains."

Now a promise made is a debt unpaid, and the trail
        has its own stern code.
In the days to come, though my lips were dumb, in
        my heart how I cursed that load.
In the long, long night, by the lone firelight, while
        the huskies, round in a ring,
Howled out their woes to the homeless snows —
        O God! how I loathed the thing.

And every day that quiet clay seemed to heavy and
        heavier grow;
And on I went, though the dogs were spent and the
        grub was getting low;

The trail was bad, and I felt half mad, but I swore I
     would not give in;
And I'd often sing to the hateful thing, and it
     hearkened with a grin.

Till I came to the marge of Lake Lebarge, and a
     derelict there lay;
It was jammed in the ice, but I saw in a trice it was
     called the "Alice May."
And I looked at it, and I thought a bit, and I looked
     at my frozen chum;
Then "Here," said I, with a sudden cry, "is my
     cre-ma-tor-eum."
Some planks I tore from the cabin floor, and I lit the
     boiler fire;
Some coal I found that was lying around, and I
     heaped the fuel higher;
The flames just soared, and the furnace roared —
     such a blaze you seldom see;
And I burrowed a hole in the glowing coal, and I
     stuffed in Sam McGee.

Then I made a hike, for I didn't like to hear him
     sizzle so;
And the heavens scowled, and the huskies howled,
     and the wind began to blow.
It was icy cold, but the hot sweat rolled down my
     cheeks, and I don't know why;
And the greasy smoke in an inky cloak went
     streaking down the sky.

I do not know how long in the snow I wrestled with
grisly fear;
But the stars came out and they danced about ere
again I ventured near;
I was sick with dread, but I bravely said: "I'll just
take a peep inside.
I guess he's cooked, and it's time I looked"; . . .
then the door I opened wide.

And there sat Sam, looking cool and calm, in the
heart of the furnace roar;
And he wore a smile you could see a mile, and
he said, "Please close the door.
It's fine in here, but I greatly fear you'll let in the
cold and storm —
Since I left Plumtree, down in Tennessee, it's the first
time I've been warm."

There are strange things done in the midnight sun
By the men who moil for gold;
The Arctic trails have their secret tales
That would make your blood run cold;

The Northern Lights have seen queer sights,
But the queerest they ever did see
Was that night on the marge of Lake Lebarge
I cremated Sam McGee.

The Spell of the Yukon

I wanted the gold, and I sought it;
I scrabbled and mucked like a slave.
Was it famine or scurvy — I fought it;
I hurled my youth into a grave.
I wanted the gold, and I got it —
Came out with a fortune last fall, —
Yet somehow life's not what I thought it,
And somehow the gold isn't all.

No! There's the land. (Have you seen it?)
It's the cussedest land that I know,
From the big, dizzy mountains that screen it
To the deep, deathlike valleys below.
Some say God was tired when He made it;
Some say it's a fine land to shun;
Maybe; but there's some as would trade it
For no land on earth — and I'm one.

You come to get rich (damned good reason);
You feel like a exile at first;
You hate it like hell for a season,
And then you are worse than the worst.
It grips you like some kinds of sinning;
It twists you from foe to a friend;
It seems it's been since the beginning;
It seems it will be to the end.

I've stood in some mighty-mouthed hollow
That's plumb-full of hush to the brim;
I've watched the big, husky sun wallow
In crimson and gold, and grow dim,

Till the moon set the pearly peaks gleaming,
And the stars tumbled out, neck and crop;
And I've thought that I surely was dreaming,
With the peace o' the world piled on top.

The summer — no sweeter was ever;
The sunshiny woods all athrill;
The grayling aleap in the river,
The bighorn asleep on the hill.

The strong life that never knows harness;
The wilds where the caribou call;
The freshness, the freedom, the farness —
O God! how I'm stuck on it all.

The winter! the brightness that blinds you,
The white land locked tight as a drum,
The cold fear that follows and finds you,
The silence that bludgeons you dumb,
The snows that are older than history,
The woods where the weird shadows slant;
The stillness, the moonlight, the mystery,
I've bade 'em good-by — but I can't.

There's land where the mountains are nameless,
And the rivers all run God knows where;
There are lives that are erring and aimless,
And deaths that just hang by a hair;
There are hardships that nobody reckons;
There are valleys unpeopled and still;
There's a land — oh, it beckons and beckons,
And I want to go back — and I will.

They're making my money diminish;
I'm sick of the taste of champagne.
Thank God! when I'm skinned to a finish
I'll pike to the Yukon again.
I'll fight — and you bet it's no sham-fight;
It's hell! — but I've been there before;
And it's better than this by a damsite —
So me for the Yukon once more.

There's gold, and it's haunting and haunting;
It's luring me on as of old;
Yet it isn't the gold that I'm wanting
So much as just finding the gold.
It's the great, big, broad land 'way up yonder,
It's the forests where silence has lease;
It's the beauty that thrills me with wonder,
It's the stillness that fills me with peace.

The Song of the Wage-Slave

When the long, long day is over, and the Big Boss
          gives me my pay,
I hope that it won't be hell-fire, as some of the
          parsons say,
And I hope that it won't be heaven, with some of the
          parsons I've met —
All I want is just quiet, just to rest and forget.
Look at my face, toil-furrowed; look at my calloused
          hands;
Master, I've done Thy bidding, wrought in Thy
          many lands —
Wrought for the little masters, big-bellied they be,
          and rich;
I've done their desire for a daily hire, and I die like a
          dog in a ditch.
I have used the strength Thou hast given, Thou
          knowest I did not shirk;
Threescore years of labor — Thine be the long day's
          work.
And now, Big Master, I'm broken and bent and
          twisted and scarred,
But I've held my job, and Thou knowest, and Thou
          will not judge me hard.
Thou knowest my sins are many, and often I've
          played the fool—
Whiskey and cards and women, they made me the
          devil's tool.
I was just like a child with money; I flung it away
          with a curse.

Feasting a fawning parasite, or glutting a harlot's purse;
Then back to the woods repentant, back to the mill
  or the mine.
I, the worker of workers, everything in my line.
Everything hard but headwork (I'd no more brains
  than a kid).
A brute with brute strength to labor, doing as I was bid;
Living in camps with men-folk, a lonely and
  loveless life;
Never knew kiss of sweetheart, never caress of wife.
A brute with brute strength to labor, and they were
  so far above —
Yet I'd gladly have gone to the gallows for one little
  look of Love.
I, with the strength of two men, savage and shy and
  wild —
Yet how I'd ha' treasured a woman, and the sweet,
  warm kiss of a child!
Well, 'tis Thy world, and Thou knowest.
  I blaspheme and my ways be rude;
But I've lived my life as I found it, and I've done
  my best to be good;
I, the primitive toiler, half naked and grimed to the eyes,
Sweating it deep in their ditches, swining it stark in
  their styes;
Hurling down forests before me, spanning
  tumultuous streams;
Down in the ditch building o'er me palaces fairer
  than dreams;

Boring the rock to the ore-bed, driving the road
      through the fen,
Resolute, dumb, uncomplaining, a man in a world
      of men.
Master, I've filled my contract, wrought in Thy
      many lands;
Not by my sins wilt Thou judge me, but by the work
      of my hands.
Master, I've done Thy bidding, and the light is low
      in the west,
And the long, long shift is over . . . Master, I've
      earned it — Rest.